Rosella

Tui

Bellbird

Waxeye

Pigeon

Morepork

Kingfisher

Greenfinch

JOURNEY THROUGH A LANDSCAPE
Paintings of New Zealand

Friends: with dogs and horse the farmer patrols his hill pastures.

JOURNEY THROUGH A LANDSCAPE
Paintings of New Zealand

by

DON NEILSON

Text by Ian F. Grant

A.H. & A.W. REED

WELLINGTON SYDNEY LONDON

First published 1975

A. H. & A. W. REED LTD.
182 Wakefield Street, Wellington
53 Myoora Road, Terrey Hills, Sydney 2084
11 Southampton Row, London WC1B 5HA
also
16 Beresford Street, Auckland
165 Cashel Street, Christchurch

ISBN: 0 589 00939 7

Set in Plantin by NZ Consolidated Press Ltd., Wellington
Printed and bound by Kyodo Printing Company Ltd., Tokyo

CONTENTS

COLOUR PLATES

Front cover: Milford Sound, clearing weather
Back cover: Pahiatua, Old stables

New Zealand: Journey Through a Landscape

On Sundays they sang lustily about building Jerusalem in England's green and pleasant land; the rest of the week, last century's pioneering European settlers were dourly dedicated to creating a green and profitable land out of New Zealand's unpromising terrain.

Today, green pastureland clambers high up steep hillsides, skirts the rivers that tumble down from the country's mountain backbone, creeps close to the hazy sweep of wide, white beaches and lingers just a few motorway minutes from city centres.

In about 100 years New Zealand's forest, fern and tussock land, largely undisturbed for thousands of years, was roughly transformed. The landscape's last, and possibly most dramatic, upheaval was pre-destined when Europe discovered the South Pacific.

OPPOSITE PAGE

Summer landscape, Northland

The fur seals, butchered in their thousands early last century
now breed in safety at Taiaroa Head near Dunedin.

Giant Kauri Waipoua Forest.

The Europeans Arrive

Towards the end of the eighteenth century, and fitfully at first, Europeans arrived in New Zealand. In 1769 and 1773, James Cook had charted the coastline with a mapmaker's skill which still astonishes. From 1788, and Sydney-town's dubious beginnings as a penal settlement, transports beat to and fro with convict cargoes. By 1790 the East India Company relaxed its monopolistic ways sufficiently to let British whalers and sealers work around Cape Horn and into the Pacific Ocean.

In the south of New Zealand sealers and bay whalers set up camp on isolated beaches, slaughtering beasts helplessly conditioned by centuries-old migratory patterns. Often the hard life was softened by "wives" matter-of-factly provided by friendly Maori chiefs, but these relationships rarely survived the end of a killing season.

In the north, even before sperm whalers interrupted their Pacific Ocean chases to pick up water casks and gulp down rough-edged rum at the grog shops along the beach at Kororareka, the towering, tough and ramrod straight trunks of the *kauri* had caught the discerning eye of many ships' captains and New Zealand spars and timbers were highly marketable commodities in deep-sea ports around the world.

Charles Heaphy, artist-draughtsman to the New Zealand Company, later noted the profitability of the kauri trade: "*The missionaries have dealt largely in this article; and some of their numbers finding the trade more profitable than their other avocations, have resigned their clerical profession, and engaged wholly in the business.*"

The northern *kauri* forests, arguably New Zealand's greatest national asset, were systematically plundered. Then, during the second half of last century, gumdiggers pockmarked the land in their search for the valuable fossilised resin remains of earlier *kauri* forests.

The European settlements founded in both main islands during the 1840s and 1850s were either directly inspired or broadly influenced by the ideas of Edward Gibbon Wakefield, famous theoretician of Britain's energetic nineteenth century colonial expansion. Very simply, Wakefield proposed the transportation of a microcosm of English society, with the landed class paying a "sufficient" price for their mixed town and country holdings to provide free passages for the artisans who would contribute the range of necessary community skills.

As usual, theory was one thing and practical considerations in untamed, heavily forested New Zealand quite another.

In 1842 one Wellington settler wrote angrily to a London newspaper complaining about the delays in land allocation. Few early colonists would have disagreed with his description of the new country: "*New*

While most of the boats and too many of the houses built from kauri are now gone, pockets of these magnificent trees remain in Northland in places inaccessible to the woodman's axe last century. A few giants still rise up to 43 metres (140 feet). *Tane Mahuta*, the god of the forest, in the Waipoua State Forest is about 1200 years old, with a girth of 13 metres (43 feet) and a sheer trunk of 18 metres (60 feet) to the first branches.

Zealand is one of the wildest places you can imagine — very mountainous, everywhere so thickly wooded that you cannot walk without a path being cut.*"

It was possible, however imperfectly, to adapt Wellington's town plan, designed in London for a billiard table terrain, to the rugged reality, but it quickly proved economically impossible to preserve the closely-knit, agricultural village communities that were an important element in Wakefield's theories.

While colonists in Wellington, Nelson, Taranaki, Wanganui, Otago and Canterbury struggled valiantly but vainly with the unworkable ideal, adventurous and ambitious squatters drove or shipped flocks of sheep to the forest-isolated, native grasslands in the Wairarapa and southern Hawkes Bay and, in the South Island, to the tussock-covered plains, downs, foothills and high country of Marlborough, Canterbury and Otago.

The full-scale human invasion of a land that was for so long uniquely without man, or even animals, had begun.

A magnificent old rimu tree towering above the bush
in the King Country, west of Taumarunui.

A Land of Mountains and Forests

MAORI MYTHOLOGY and hard-nosed geologists agree about one thing: New Zealand did rise from the sea. But while Maori legend has that man-of-all-miracles, Maui, fishing up the North Island with his own blood as bait and his grandmother's jawbone as hook, scientists now claim, with considerable confidence but excusable lack of precision, that the country, once possibly part of a massive Tasmantis continent, sank beneath the sea between 30–130 million years ago and then gradually reappeared, up to a mere million or so years back, as today's North, South and Stewart Islands.

The two main islands are a little larger than Great Britain — but there the geographical similarity ends. While Britain is crowded, almost smothered, by Europe, New Zealand's islands rise out of a lonely sea.

Few countries in the world are more physically alone than New Zealand. The nearest neighbour, Australia, is as far away as Leningrad is from London. Further away to the north-west are stepping-stone archipelagos leading to Asia, to the north-east the parsimonious sprinkling of Pacific islands, to the east, over an endless succession of horizons, South America, and to the south the frozen wastes of Antarctica.

Isolation is, for those who admire brevity, New Zealand's one-word story. Well over half the country's vegetation is found nowhere else, evolving alone since the peaks of the great, sunken South Pacific continent heaved above the long ocean swell. Before Polynesian sailors landed dogs and rats, the only mammals were bats, carried to New Zealand on the prevailing westerly breezes, and seals which included the hospitable coastline in their migratory travels.

New Zealand became one of the world's most spectacular aviaries when ocean birds rested along the coast, migratory birds discovered the islands and returned, and other birds, many of them later forgetting how to fly, fluttered down exhausted after flights of thousands of miles in search of land after capricious winds had blown them out onto empty seas.

New Zealand was one of the last Pacific landfalls made by the daring and skilful Polynesian navigators, possibly because its long, narrow islands run roughly north to south. The South Pacific was also one of the last blanks to be filled in by European mapmakers.

Today, the vast ocean around her insulates New Zealand, absorbing and mixing the stifling heat funneling off central Australia and the freezing winds from Antarctica, to produce a pleasant sunny, temperate climate with the consistent rainfall that gives New Zealand's pastoral landscape its freshly-painted look. Today, despite jet travel, isolation remains the favourite, brooding theme of New Zealand poets and novelists.

Towards the end of the epoch of rebirth, endless slipping and thrusting along fault lines gradually built New Zealand's impressive mountain chains — the Southern Alps, Kaikouras and North Island ranges. Wind and water erosion during endless centuries have softened the topography of many peaks and valleys, but there are still many dramatically sharp-edged reminders of the country's geologically young landscape.

During the same period glacial and volcanic activity created different North and South Island landscapes.

As countless ice ages touched and retreated from southern New Zealand the comings and goings of great glaciers gouged out the rugged Westland valleys, scoured mountain sides and dug lakes and fiords that plunged 200 feet (61 metres) below sea level.

The wild beauty of the Tongariro National Park with Mt Ngauruhoe smoking in the background.

More than half the North Island was covered by outpourings of lava or wind-blown ash, scoria and pumice. When the hot ash and pumice glass fragments from the most violent eruptions, between Mt. Ruapehu and the Bay of Plenty, cooled they formed a thick mass of rock covering nearly 26,000 square kilometres (10,000 square miles). Today, the rainbow-splashed cuttings on roadsides between Taupo and Gisborne signpost at least five different volcanic strata.

Apart from the rise in sea level which drowned some valleys at the end of the glacial period and a final, testy pumice shower falling in a massive arc around Lake Taupo less than 2,000 years ago, the last 10,000 years were — at least until the coming of man — comparatively tranquil.

The making of New Zealand was complete. Mountains covered four-fifths of the South Island. While only one-fifth of the North Island was truly mountainous, the remainder was mostly hill country, plateau and down-land. Even the lowlands were broken and hilly.

New Zealand's far north was a narrow, jagged peninsula of low

Ski huts on the northern face of Mt Ruapehu.

15

"The Pinnacles" at Cape Palliser — Nature's own cathedral-like erosion at the North Island's southernmost point.

forested hill country and mangrove tidal estuaries. Harbours on opposite sides of the peninsula lapped a narrow isthmus which widened again to the swampy Hauraki plains and peaty Waikato River basin, both scrub and fern covered.

The island's vast central plateau was, and is, a grab-bag of nature's freaks with Rotorua's rivers of hot water and the underground glow-worm grottos at Waitomo. South of Taupo, a lake of inland sea proportions, manuka and bracken struggled forlornly. Due west of the volcanoes — Ruapehu, Ngauruhoe and Tongariro — lined up in generally quiet contemplation of their earlier handiwork, Mt. Egmont looked down on the Taranaki lowlands and the dense forests that swept eastward and then south to the bottom of the island.

The North Island's mountain chain lay to the east, a narrow, ragged line of ranges running from East Cape to Cook Strait. On the north-eastern slopes of the mountains, forests darkened the steeply corrugated hills falling away to the sea. Further south the forest opened into scrubland.

16

PLATE 1.   Kapiti Island, Wellington

With a pause at Cook Strait, the mountains surged down the South Island's western flank, tussock grasses replacing dull green rain forest. Along the Southern Alps' stony ranges, divided by deep glacial valleys, the tussock merged with green-black beech forests which halted below snow-covered, rock ridges.

In the far south-west corner of the island, dripping-wet mountain forests climbed up and down canyons that became fiords when they met the sea. Eastwards, and boxed in on three sides, the arid, desertscape of Central Otago's mountain basins was sometimes relieved by the breathtaking blueness of glacial lakes.

West of the Southern Alps, clouds and forest were in a permanent embrace well down hillsides that careered head-over-heels to the sea. East of the ranges, yellow-brown tussock grasslands sloped slowly across shingle plains, dissected by mile-wide river trenches, to the sea 110 kilometres (seventy miles) away.

Before man's appearance practically all of New Zealand, except for the bare mountain tops and tussock, scrub and fernlands, was covered with forest.

Dense evergreen forests followed the coastline, usually with a scrub or sand-dune buffer in between, and enveloped inland hills and valleys. Broadleaf coastal forest trees rarely climbed above 11 metres (36 feet), but a particularly robust *pohutukawa* might heave itself another 6 metres (20 feet) into the air to show off its red-flecked summer foliage.

In the great inland forests there was a clear three-level hierarchy. Isolated conifers would tower above the irregular umbrella tops of 27 metres (90 feet) tall broadleafs like *tawa* and *rata*, with smaller shade-stunted trees, shrubs and tree ferns far below. In the northern North Island the majestic *kauri*, wearing an imperious crown of branches on top of a sheer trunk that might soar 55 metres (180 feet) high, dominated the forests. Further south, *matai* and *totara* were prominent conifers, and *rimu* forests spilled down the West Coast terraces.

The beech forests, which preferred the South Island's cooler mountain slopes and lowlands, were quite different in appearance. As the climate restricted these forests to one or more beech species there was a single layer of trees and a more open forest floor.

Mighty rimu trunks in the Tararuas.

Looking across Lake Pukaki to Mt Cook National Park from the Mackenzie Country.

19

Opposite: A mountain pool high in the Tararua Range, bordering the Wairarapa.

PLATE 2.   Homeward bound, South Wairarapa

The well-preserved *Tapeka* carved meeting house at Waihi village on the south-western shore of Lake Taupo.

The First New Zealanders

ARCHAEOLOGICAL EVIDENCE suggests that about 3,000 years ago the first New Zealanders tentatively explored an environment totally foreign to a simple culture that had evolved on hot, lush Pacific Islands.

They found the dark and damp North Island forests quite alien, the interior a volcanic desert. Finally they settled in the drier, sunnier east coast lowlands of the South Island.

They found a prolific bird life which, without animals to prey on them or compete for food, had responded in exotic, even unique ways. A number of species forgot how to fly — including the kiwi, New Zealand's doubtfully appropriate national emblem. Another species grew to enormous size. The moa was often three-and-a-half metres (twelve feet) tall from reptilian toes to the top of an ostrich-like head and weighed as much as the prize bulls that shake the ground in country show rings today. Great herds grazed the coastal grasslands in the South Island.

In their own primitive ways, the moa hunters, as the first settlers are called today, decimated the moa herds as systematically as the white men eliminated the buffalo from the plains of North America.

In a stern and unyielding environment, the moa was a conveniently packaged answer to man's survival problems: food, clothing, fish hooks, spears. Even the moa eggs — which could be 254 mm (10 ins) long — made excellent water carriers.

In a few hundred years the clumsy, flightless moa, which had evolved to comical proportions over countless thousands of years, was close to extinction and the moa hunters were burning millions of acres of *matai* and *totara* forests across the Canterbury plains in an increasingly desperate flushing out of surviving birds.

There were probably never more than 10–20,000 moa hunters and they have left few mementos of their meagre culture. But they did leave a massive memorial to their South Island occupation: native grasses fanning out to cover the dismal skeletons of the majestic, primeval forests, and a further thirty-nine bird species wiped out in the frantic search for food after the moa's disappearance.

During the long era of disputed land rights last century, Papawai rivalled Ngaruawahia, headquarters of the Maori King movement, as the principal centre of Maori influence. When the Maori King movement failed, Papawai's spiritual importance increased — and the *teko teko*'s facing inward was a symbolic attempt to jolt a beaten, dejected race out of its lethargy. Traditionally, *teko teko* faced outward to scare away enemies — at Papawai they faced inward, confronting the defeatists who prophesied the end of Maoridom.

After the bush was burnt and the stumps removed,
the ground was ready for ploughing.

Opening up the South

A THOUSAND YEARS later, a number of European settlers also favoured the
eastern plains, downs and foothills of the South Island. The moa hunters
had helpfully cleared the forests and, more convenient still, had not
survived to argue land titles as the Maoris were doing with North Island
colonists, who stayed frustratingly hemmed in by the disputed forests.

The early runholders of Canterbury and Otago, often more familiar
with Latin verbs than farming practice, regularly burnt massive tracts
of leasehold tussock and scrubland charcoal black in autumn and grazed
their flocks on the bright green spring shoots.

Charles Tripp and John Acland, the young English lawyers who
established and, to some extent, tamed the famous Mt. Peel station, were
typical of the early South Island squatters. In March 1856 alone, they
burned off 50,000 acres, Acland penning his diary in the firelight and the
flames leaping so high they could be clearly seen 60 miles (nearly 100 km)
away in Christchurch.

By the 1860s the romantic, amateur era had faded: runholders were
buying up their leases at low prices introduced to assist small farmers
onto the land; they were building the nostalgically English manor houses
with the high initial profits from the careless exploitation of the native
pastures; they were experimenting with sheep breeds and streamlining

24

PLATE 3.   Governor's Bay and Port Hills

Remains of a gold miner's cottage near Cromwell.

shearing techniques; they were shrewdly protecting their substantial interests by playing an active part in the colony's political life.

Just when it looked as if falling wool prices and devastated tussock pastures would slow the south's progress, gold was discovered in Otago and then on the West Coast.

The man who started the gold rushes, Gabriel Read, later wrote: "... the prospects began to brighten, just when I had deemed it meet to make a flit for my tent, as darkness was coming on the scene. At a place where a kind of road crossed on a shallow bar, I shovelled away about $2\frac{1}{2}$ feet of gravel, arrived at a beautiful soft slate and saw the gold shining like the stars in Orion on a dark frosty night."

Stories spread of miners at Gabriel's Gully tearing up tussock clumps and shaking nuggets from the roots, and others, elsewhere on the goldfields, making moderate fortunes from claims the size of suburban sitting-rooms. Otago's population sky-rocketed five-fold in two years.

Not that the miners treated the landscape with any more care than the fire-stick pastoralists. Pits were scooped out of promising gullies and flats and the blue and yellow topsoil roughly heaped nearby; rivers were

26

dammed and streams diverted; gold-bearing terraces were cut, blasted and tunnelled.

Otago's alluvial gold had petered out by the early 1870s but many of the miners, wearying of a fortune-hunt that had begun on the Californian or Victorian fields, turned their hardened and practical hands to farming.

Gabriel Read died a pauper in a Tasmanian old men's home, but gold catapulted Dunedin straight from stagnating township to soberly substantial city of unrivalled commercial importance, consolidated the South Island's economic domination of the colony for a further two decades, and helped underwrite the spectacular attack on the North Island forests.

Today, and more so than on the West Coast where the lush vegetation quickly covered the diggings, Otago's drier climate has preserved reminders of its most spectacular decade: scarred terraces and hillsides, water races leading nowhere and monster piles of tailings from the clanking dredges that scoured the river bottoms for years after the dish and shovel miners had gone.

But Central Otago's stark, broken hills are now softened by green pasture, irrigated orchards of peaches and apricots on river terraces and by the autumnal reds and golds of gracious English trees.

There has been a revolution in high country management techniques, but little else has changed on the South Island runs — the monotonous greys and browns of the tussock grass are occasionally broken by a cluster of red-roofed farm buildings stockaded by pine trees, the isolated headquarters of sheep runs that sprawl to the horizon and beyond and use rocky gorges and wide river beds to fence in sparse flocks of fine-wool merinos.

A gold dredge operating in South Westland.

27

Old farm water wheel near Ashburton.

Some of the runs are as big as they were in the 1850s when Lawrence Kennaway applied at the land office in Christchurch for the country ". . . bounded on the north by the northernmost branch of the River Hakatere — on the south, by a second branch of the same river — westward, by a black birch forest and the base of the snowy ranges — and eastward, to the extent required."

Molesworth, now government owned, covers half-a-million acres, and it takes a dozen men nearly two months to muster the station's sheep.

High country mustering remains New Zealand's toughest job. It's all part of an autumn day's work for musterers to scramble hundreds of feet up and down loose shingle faces and treacherous scree slopes in bitter, numbing cold to flush out a few more tardy sheep.

Yet there are high country compensations: frost-white flowers suddenly opening in this bleak, stark landscape; mile upon mile of tussock glowing luminously at sunset.

On the Canterbury plains the tawny tussock grass that swept down from the Southern Alps has become the country's most varied and colourful landscape. As the seasons pass and the large, gorse-sheltered fields are carefully rotated, thousands of lowland acres are a constantly changing kaleidoscope of plough-furrowed purple-brown soil, rippling waves of golden wheat, the bright green of heavy pea crops and the more sombre green of fat lamb grazing pastures.

PLATE 4.   Mackenzie Plains, South Canterbury

Old rimu tree, Mt Egmont National Park.

The First Conservationists

THE MOA HUNTERS searched for food on the Canterbury plains; the Maoris who followed them to New Zealand found that the food crops they brought — kumara, taro, yam and gourd — prospered in the northern, sub-tropical parts of New Zealand.

The Maoris were much more aggressive than the moa hunters, particularly after successful adaptation to their new environment gave them the time to develop both martial and peaceful arts.

Yet, ironically, the Maoris treated the landscape, particularly the forests, with more care and respect than either the moa hunters before them or the yeoman farmers from Europe who followed.

They were, in however limited a sense, New Zealand's first conservationists.

Again myth and science are at odds, but whether by planned, epic voyages or storm-blown accident, the Maoris arrived from the Society Islands several thousand miles to the north-east during the thirteenth and fourteenth centuries.

A solid majority of the Maori population, peaking at about 250,000 in pre-European days, tended their gardens, mostly temporary ones in forest clearings, in Northland, Auckland and the Bay of Plenty. South of Lake Taupo to Banks Peninsula midway down the South Island, Maori communities were forced to find other staple foods: fish, birds, forest berries and fern roots.

Despite the sightings of inland fires regularly logged by the explorers, whalers and sealers who sailed, surveyed and exploited the New Zealand coastline during the late eighteenth and early nineteenth centuries, the Maoris did not devastate the North Island forests.

For one thing, the dense, dripping forest smothered fires lit to clear kumara patches or to fatten fern roots. Then, unlike the moa hunters, the Maoris understood the importance of the great rain forests to their culture and survival.

Tane, god of the forest, strode authoritatively through the Maori myths giving a sanctity to an asset that provided *kauri* and *kahikatea* tree boles for laborious adzing into canoes, bark for colourful dyes, long vines to fashion into eel-pots, and berries, fruit, stems and shoots, rats and birds to add variety to a starchy diet.

There is even evidence that Maoris established colonies of *weka*, large, flightless rail, on deserted off-shore islands to become, in time, brimming larders. Similarly, they stocked inland lakes and streams with fish and eels.

During the early Maori period the lighter coastal forests, warmed by the sea breezes, were accidentally or purposely fired, and scrub, tussock grass and bracken grew in their place.

But inland a trained eye is often needed to see the Maori impact. The Maoris were great travellers — exploring, trading and later waging the inter-tribal warfare that was, at least until the European musket added a deadlier purpose, a mixture of prideful revenge and the almost universal masculine love of rough and tumble sport. Although narrow tracks ran along valley floors and over dividing hills and ranges to Taranaki and deep into the interior, the Maoris canoed whenever possible. They took their canoes up and down the protected eastern coastline of the North Auckland peninsula and on the Waikato River and its tributaries rising in the central mountain chains. On the west coast it was simplest to march along the wide, safe beaches.

In the north, even today, hundreds of hills are mute, carved monuments to the warfare that drove Maori tribes into fortified *pas* on top of terraced slopes.

Then there are the signs of bustling, agricultural enterprise. Great gravel pits were excavated to mix shingle with heavy clay soils — more than 2,000 hectares (5,000 acres) of soil was enriched in the mid-Waikato plain alone; whole hillsides were burrowed full of storage pits for surplus kumara.

31

The King Country: on the road from Taumarunui to New Plymouth dense virgin bush.

32

The North's Bush Burns

IN THE early years of the nineteenth century possibly two-thirds of the North Island were still bush-covered, the rest a muddle of scrub, tussock and fern. By 1840, when the first colonists gazed with horrified fascination at the dense bush spilling down to the water's edge in Wellington's great land-locked harbour, forests probably occupied no more than half the island, with the destruction of the northern *kauri* forests already well advanced.

Thirty years later a partially successful attempt had been made to overlay the coastal and native grassland landscapes with the neatness and order of the English countryside. But the ancient, dark, Rangitikei, Manawatu, southern Hawkes Bay and Wairarapa forests had scarcely been touched.

Years of uncertainty about settler titles to Maori land bartered during the early, infectious buying and selling sprees were not resolved until after the bloody Maori Wars fought during the 1860s in the Waikato and Taranaki. With a growing population eager to move out of its coastal enclaves, the government anxious for development that would put a healthy jingle back into a public purse emptied during the costly wars, and South Island money-men sniffing out investment possibilities, the scene was set for the massive attack on the North Island forests over the next thirty years.

Colonial treasurer Vogel, with a daring that left his admirers breathless and opponents speechless, raised £10 million for a neatly dovetailing immigration and public works programme to link the still isolated North Island settlements and open up the interior: the immigrants were to hack and burn narrow passages through the forest, lay the roads and rail tracks and buy, out of their wages, 40-acre lots along the route.

Norwegian immigrant families tackled the Seventy Mile Bush, which blocked the overland route between Wellington and Napier, from both

The King Country: rough burnt-over pastures a sad contrast with the virgin bush shown on page 32.

the Wairarapa and southern Hawkes Bay sides. It was the densest forest in New Zealand and the massive stands of *totara*, *rimu* and *matai* awed and obsessed the bush settlers who lived in rough whares in the semi-darkness of claustrophobic clearings.

Wives and children cleared the undergrowth on the farm lots and husbands felled the trees on days away from the work gangs. Forest cut in the winter months and dried during the hot summers was fired in February and March. The ash-fertilised soil was hand-sown and cattle grazed the coarse grasses. Later, horse teams dragged out rotting stumps and heaps of charred tree remains were re-fired. Finally it was possible to plough, re-grass or crop the land. Scandinavian bush settlers were often so poor that a decade might pass before they could afford a horse, which was then prominently posed in family portrait photographs sent to relatives in Norway.

Although it was soon obvious that the bush settlers could not survive on 40-acre incomes, their years of loneliness and hardship were not completely wasted: the men who survived apprenticeships of un-controlled fires, swollen rivers and crashing trees became experts with the axe and crosscut saw and were in continuing demand as more and more North Island forests were felled and fired.

Northland's forests had at least been shaped into spars and ships' timber, substantial houses and sturdy furniture; many millions of handsomely grained hardwood trees felled in the three closing decades of last century burnt or rotted where they crashed to the ground.

The enthusiastic bush clearance programme of the 1870s grew to frenzied proportions in the 1880s when the government's vague hopes for the interior's potential were suddenly given a sharp, exciting focus with the successful London sale of sheep carcasses after a ninety-three day voyage from Dunedin in the makeshift refrigerated hold aboard a wool clipper.

The native pastures of the South Island hill country were struggling — their humus layers depleted by repeated burnings — to support thirteen million sheep bred primarily for their wool. So the hopes for a large and prosperous trade in frozen meat, butter and cheese largely depended on opening up the North Island's interior.

After the doldrums of the 1870s, and the prospect of swapping the one or two shillings offered for a sheep at the nearest boiling-down works for the heady £1 or more paid for a frozen carcass in London, it was understandable that the farmers grassed every last inch of available land.

Much of the North Island's hill country pastureland refuses to be completely tamed. It is deeply notched with gorges and wrinkled with hundreds of narrow, tumbling streams and blackened, ghostly reminders of last century's forests still stalk the skyline. A large number of New Zealand's sheep are bred on this steeply up-and-down landscape; huge woolsheds often crowd modest homesteads on the limited near-flat land.

Dairy country, once lowland forest in Taranaki, swamp in the Waikato basin and peaty flats on the Hauraki plains has a much more man-made look to it. Small, lush-green paddocks are tidily hedged in boxthorn or barberry and sheltered by pine tree stands. Modern, almost suburban, farm bungalows and highly efficient herring-bone cowsheds underline the high productivity of the lush, imported pasture grasses on these compact farms that are rarely larger than 50 hectares (123 acres).

The North Island's thermal region of volcanoes, mud pools and geysers has been well-enough behaved to become the linch-pin of a fast-growing tourist trade. Two mountains, Ruapehu and Ngauruhoe, occasionally smoke-signal that they are active, though sedate, old-age pensioners. There has been only one disaster in European times. In 1886 Mount Tarawera, in the Bay of Plenty, literally blew its top, a gigantic nine mile long crack opening across the mountain. One hundred Maoris were killed by the stones and boiling mud that rained down on villages as far as sixteen kilometres (ten miles) away.

The pumice lands, once considered too poor for grazing, have become the centre of a huge new timber industry. Battered Mount Tarawera overlooks the first exotic forests, planted early this century when it was realised that very little of the remaining native bush could be milled economically.

Natives can take up to 200 years to develop into mature trees so pines, particularly the North American *pinus radiata*, were planted. They liked the New Zealand climate, reaching sawmill size in twenty-five to thirty years.

Today well over one million acres (404,686 ha) of pine trees march over the hills and valleys with military precision, foliage identical and, appropriately, battle-dress green. The new forests could not be more different from the wild, chaotic profusion of the indigenous forest.

36

PLATE 5. Abandoned Cottage, South Westland

On the site of a well-known old coaching stables in Greytown's main street, "Cobblestones" is an early colonial museum preserving the Wairarapa's past.

38

England in the South Seas

IN 1872 Anthony Trollope brought his novelist's eye and imagination on a visit to New Zealand, recording with mock dismay that he had not met any cannibals and had sailed right around the world without being able to escape from England.

He was, of course, exaggerating. Nevertheless, the early settlers, confronted with volcanoes, tussock grasslands, rain forests and flightless birds had worked hard, and with some success by the 1870s, to create another England in the South Seas.

Britain's pastureland was a green mantle thrown over hills and valleys alike, so it was natural to try to produce an antipodean mirror image of the old country. Britain's forest glades and open fields were filled with animals and birds strangely, even disturbingly, absent in New Zealand. What was more natural than to recreate the comfortably familiar in a country where leaping geysers and mokoed Maori faces were still alien to European eyes?

On one auspicious day in the early 1860s Major-General George Whitmore delivered to the manager of his Hawkes Bay farm a number of rabbits (with careful instructions that they be released well away from the homestead vegetable garden), eleven blackberry cuttings, pheasants, bees, and thousands of gorse plants.

Before farmers and legislators realised that they had — with a mix of habit, nostalgia and ignorance — under-estimated the differences between the two countries, poor land management and the unexpected behaviour of introduced animals was eroding, flooding and destroying pasture at an alarming rate.

At the time, of course, the rough bush frontier was a once-in-a-lifetime opportunity for slashing, burning settlers to realise their dreams of property and capital. They were guided by their experience; they had neither the time nor the inclination to question their values or methods.

Now, with the help of a century's hindsight, their mistakes are obvious. Britain's highest mountains are hillocks by New Zealand standards. The crumpled paper topography of New Zealand's high country was beyond the experience of most of the pioneer farmers. Also, and equally important, Britain's pastures had slowly unfolded since feudal times and before; they were not bludgeoned into being during a few short decades.

Very simply, much of New Zealand's young and unstable landscape could not cope with the sudden, brutal transformation.

TO PUT ON RECORD THAT

MICHAEL JOHN BURKE

A GRADUATE OF DUBLIN UNIVERSITY
AND THE FIRST OCCUPIER OF

RAINCLIFF STN

ENTERED THIS PASS KNOWN TO THE
MAORIS AS TE KOPI OPAU

IN 1855.

— // —

O YE WHO ENTER THE PORTALS OF THE
MACKENZIE TO FOUND HOMES, TAKE
THE WORD OF A CHILD OF THE MISTY
GORGES AND PLANT FOREST TREES
FOR YOUR LIVES; SO SHALL YOUR
MOUNTAIN RANGES AND RIVER FLATS
BE PRESERVED TO YOUR CHILDRENS
CHILDREN AND FOR EVERMORE,

1917

THIS PASS IS 2200 FEET
ABOVE SEA LEVEL

Despite the prophetic warning on the monument at the entrance to Burkes Pass, the Mackenzie Country has few trees, thereby allowing erosion to increase.

Hillsides Slip and Slide

PARTICULARLY in cloud-shrouded high country, the hill sides were defenceless after the forests had gone. They had been like blotting paper, absorbing the heavy, persistent rainfall, water trickling through the foliage canopy, down tree trunks, and slowly through the moss-spongy, leaf-littered forest floor to the soil below. Without the forests, the rain pounded the soil loose and it slipped, slid, avalanched into mountain streams. Rocks and boulders, their soil binding gone, crashed into the already swollen streams. Rivers, flooded by tributary streams, burst their banks in valleys below, burying pasture or cropland in silt and stones, and washing fertile soil to the sea.

During the first forty years of this century the forest-cleared hill sides in moderate to heavy rainfall areas have been pockmarked, scarred and corrugated with slips and slides as struggling, overgrazed pasture has been unable to resist the driving, beating, eroding force of rain and wind. Just before the First World War it was noted, but no more, that hundreds of acres of hillside were slumping into valley bottoms in east coast North Island districts.

Sometimes the cavalier clearance of lowland forests had equally serious consequences. On the South Island's wet west coast the removal of impressive *rimu* forests has been followed by ugly, unproductive bogs.

It took disasters like the Esk River flood in the Hawkes Bay in 1938, which ripped trees and boulders from hillsides and buried farms under two metres (six feet) of silt, to prove that only the re-forestation of watersheds and much more carefully controlled grazing of the high country could ease the problem at its source.

Shortly afterwards a national soil conservation programme began: in the last thirty years millions of tussock country, hill country and lowland acres have been brought back to life again and about twenty million hillside seedling trees and river-bank poplars and willows planted.

PLATE 6.   Wanaka aspect, Otago

The red stag: hunted by sportsmen and conservationists.
Below: Captain Cook and other early South Pacific explorers brought the first wild, island pigs to New Zealand.

The Animal Invasion

ANIMALS were introduced to New Zealand from the earliest days of European contact: to barter with the Maoris, as antidotes to homesickness, to hunt for sport, and to control other, already imported species.

But New Zealand's fauna and flora had evolved in complete isolation for millions of years: without animal predators many native birds lost the use of their wings; forests had no reason to adapt, like their European counterparts, to the browsing and rooting habits of deer, goats and pigs.

With last century's animal introductions, a number of unique bird species have disappeared; forests have been devastated; precariously grassed hill country has eroded away; rich pastureland has been destroyed.

The early explorers and whalers landed pigs and goats as gifts or in exchange for water and wood, and black and brown rats deserted when ships were pulled ashore for careening. The black rat, particularly, spread over the landscape eating fruit, berries, bird eggs and chicks in the trees it nested in.

But it has been the deliberate not the accidental animal importations that have most upset nature's delicate balance in New Zealand. It is a long and varied list: cat, rabbit, ferret, stoat, weasel, opossum, pig, goat, and deer.

Ships' cats were off-loaded at temporary shore whaling stations to deal with the native rats attracted by the smoking try-pots; pioneer settlers took cats into the deepest forest and loneliest tussock country, as pets and rat-catchers. Left to fend for themselves, or deserted, they multiplied on rich diets of slow-moving, fearless and flightless native birds.

Early nineteenth century New Zealand was a bleak exile, barely mitigated by native quail more like sitting ducks, and wild pigs, for settlers infected with the British passion for game hunting.

Wild goats devour everything the_y

The rabbit was the first of the sporting imports and, without natural enemies to hold numbers in check, bred itself to invasion proportions by the 1870s, particularly in the Canterbury tussock country where it nibbled the sprouting spring grass shoots and burrowed under the shelter of tussock clumps.

In desperation, the authorities released large numbers of ferrets, stoats and weasels — rabbit predators in Europe. They spread quickly, dining on the tame native birds that were much easier prey than scampering rabbits.

The cat, ferret, stoat and weasel and humans ate their way through several unique native bird species last century and brought others close to extinction.

Charles Heaphy echoed early settler sentiments: "*The wood pigeon is in New Zealand very large — far above the size of that in England. The plumage of the bird is very beautiful and the flesh is excellent. I have not unfrequently killed a dozen of them from one tree, so little alarm do they show at the report of a gun . . . All the other forest birds, and their numbers and variety are immense, are eatable, and generally of excellent flavour and delicacy.*"

The small, inquisitive, partridge-like native quail, with its token wing flutters, had been wiped out by cats (with the help of hungry pioneers) by 1870. Maori chiefs once wore the feathers of the branch-hopping *huia*, with its sweeping tail and ivory-coloured beak. The bird was butchered after the musket's introduction and finally exterminated by four-legged predators. The olive, brown and white New Zealand thrush, a familiar sight around the gold rush camp sites in the 1860s, has not been seen since 1955; the laughing owl, which once yelped and shrieked in the depths of the forest, was last sighted in 1914.

The notornis, or *takahe*, had been thought extinct for fifty years when a colony of these large native moorhens was discovered in a mountain valley high above Lake Te Anau in 1948. Predators certainly hastened the demise of the notornis, clumsy-looking with its massive, bright red bill, but have not been the primary cause. Naturalists believe that the birds, unable to adjust to a warmer climate, progressively retreated with their cool tussock-land habitat after the last ice age.

The green and yellow, owlish-looking *kakapo* was plentiful enough in the South Island high country to add variety to the dry-tack diet of explorers and gold miners. Today, perhaps a dozen of these flightless, ground-nesting parrots survive in a remote Fiordland valley, protected from stoat, weasel and rat predators by sheer 2100 m (about 7000 ft) cliffs.

The native parrots are all in danger of disappearing. The impudent *kea*, at one time a suspected sheep killer with a price on its olive-green head, is a soaring, swooping flier but nests in easily-raided holes and crevices on the ground. The *kea* has maintained a stronghold in Southland but the *kaka*, a forest parrot, has not adapted to exotic forests and is disappearing with its natural habitat.

Other forest dwellers like parakeets, the velvet and yellow, nectar-eating stitchback and glossy-black, orange-wattled saddleback are rarely or never seen on the mainland, with their remaining hope for survival New Zealand's off-shore bird sanctuaries.

The inquisitive *kea*.

The *takahe*, or notornis, is on the brink of extinction.

PLATE 7.   Old stone buildings, Queenstown

Thar browse the mountain tops.

Opposite: Heavily eroded domain of the thar, Arthur's Pass, Southern Alps.

Sporting colonists, not satisfied with rabbit shooting, studied deer breeds in other countries and shipped in Scottish red deer, Japanese deer, North American moose, Virginia deer and rusa deer from Java.

Except in northern *kauri* forests, the red deer has thrived in native and exotic bushland throughout the country. These versatile deer will contentedly graze tussock grass, particularly in summer, and browse the predominantly evergreen native trees and shrubs below the snow-line. Close grazing of new grass and plant growth, the sharp ground-cutting edges of hooves and heavy rain result in soil and scree avalanches that scar hillsides and fill valleys with rubble. In bush country the deer's relentless browsing of seedling trees halts forest regeneration and leads, eventually, to a rough pasture landscape.

Early this century the cliff-climbing alpine thar and chamois were introduced. Without any high altitude enemies, the thar has browsed clear the sparse cover of mountain tops along the Southern Alps and the chamois has moved, with even greater agility, throughout the South Island's alpine terrain.

A century earlier wild pigs — "Captain Cookers" because the explorer had released some — ate native ground birds as they moved into the interior, but they clearly preferred fern roots, grubs and berries.

46

The opossum systematically eats bark
and tender tree leaves.

Goats, widely used last century to keep down weeds and poisonous plants on large sheep runs, escaped into the bush and high country devouring everything they found from tussock to tree bark.

The brush-tailed opossum from Australia has probably done as much as any animal to destroy the New Zealand bush. It arrived last century, billed as a potentially profitable fur producer, and quickly spread through the country, except for the far north. Wooden power poles now carry metal discs to stop this cat-size, climbing marsupial from triggering electricity black-outs, but there has been no similarly simple method of preventing the opossum from killing forest with the systematic stripping and eating of bark and tender, growing, tree-top foliage.

After World War II a vigorous rabbit killing programme had spectacular results: farm income on infected land climbed half a billion dollars in the decade from 1958. Opossums and deer lost their protected status. Today, commercial hunters are shooting thousands of deer in remote South Island forests, helicoptering out the carcasses which become, finally and profitably, venison steaks on West German dining room tables. But, as herd survivors are driven into new, even more isolated areas, there is likely to be greater rather than less forest damage.

Although rabbit, magpie and gorse introductions are liberally cursed today, there have been some successful immigrants. Hedgehogs eat slugs and grubs rather than the bird eggs favoured by their European cousins; brown and rainbow trout have grown big in empty rivers and lakes and the country now has an international reputation for its fishing; the skylark, blackbird and chaffinch contribute harmoniously to the bird song chorus that greets the New Zealand dawn.

PLATE 8. Pohutukawa tree, Whitianga

Beech forest vista Lake Manapouri.

The Landscape Today

IT IS NOW easy to criticise the destruction of the forests and the introduction of animals that further decimated the native bird life and further weakened precarious hillsides, particularly as New Zealand's latter-day ecology-consciousness is largely derived from the secure prosperity of an export trade pioneered by last century's single-minded farmers.

Yet the almost complete transformation of the New Zealand landscape from wild tussock, scrub and towering forests to neatly fenced, bright green pastureland in little more than a century was a human achievement that dwarfs today's gigantic hydroelectric power schemes.

Perhaps it is too much of a simplification to consider New Zealand one huge farm, but it is true that nearly ninety per cent of the country's export income is earned from agricultural produce; that farm livestock outnumber three million New Zealanders by about fifty to one at the height of the breeding season; that farm land covers two-thirds of New Zealand.

Last century dense forest covered the rich dairy country encircling Mt Egmont.

PLATE 9.   King Country farmlands

Today, with a temperate climate that encourages all-year-round pasture growth, the lavish sowing of white clover — a grass that literally gulps down production-boosting nitrogen — and annual injections of superphosphate and lime by the million tons, New Zealand farmers outproduce, acre by acre, their counterparts anywhere in the world.

Total farm output has doubled since the 1930s, mainly because of the aeroplane's contribution to the gradual repair of the badly-eroded, back-block hill country landscape. Experiments during and immediately after World War II showed that aerial top dressing was practical. Enthusiastic farmers bulldozed landing strips on their properties; demobbed pilots and surplus wartime planes teamed up to service the aerial top dressing boom.

Soon stubby, single-engined planes on their hilltop-skimming fertiliser and insecticide "bombing" runs were as familiar a sight as stainless steel milk tankers bowling along country roads. On fine days, when winds were light and variable, the planes flew from daylight into the deep twilight sowing seed on burnt-off tussock country, dusting

Bringing in the hay, cut and
baled for winter feed.

pastures with fertiliser, shovelling out tons of poisoned carrots over
rabbit-infested land, and dropping fencing material with pinpoint
precision.

As time passes the skeletal remains of the forests disappear from the
hill country pastures, tussock is replaced with green, luscious grasses,
swamps are drained. The pastoral landscape looks more domesticated,
like a giant's vast, manicured lawn.

In time scarred slopes heal, except in areas like the Wairarapa's
Aorangi Mountains where pigs, goats, deer and opossum have methodi-
cally destroyed the vegetation from the undergrowth to the tree tops,
leaving a dead and dying forest and endemic soil erosion.

Nearly ninety per cent of the native bush has gone but it still appears,
unexpectedly, running riot up a valley too steep-sided to farm. More
than two million hectares (five million acres) survive in national parks,
with their bush tracks, tramping huts and camp sites. Fiordland, with
its three million acres of rain forest, unscaled mountains, icy lakes and
perpendicular fiords, is among the world's largest national parks.

Clean, cool water tumbles down a cliffside
to join the river below.

Last century most of the magnificent North Island native forests were destroyed without question; today the milling of the surviving indigenous forest, particularly South Island beech, is subject to lively public debate.

The wild and primitive force of the rocky seashore is enduring, the mountains remain comparatively aloof from progress, but New Zealand's streams, rivers and lakes are in danger.

Ironically, the greatest threat to New Zealand's fast-flowing rivers and limpid lakes are the scores of millions of tons of fertiliser and insecticide that coaxed spectacular results from the country's pastures during the last three decades. Some lakes are in danger of choking from the algae that multiply dramatically on the nutrients in fertiliser run-off.

In the 1970s the country's prosperity still rides on the backs of sheep and cattle, but only four per cent of all New Zealanders actually farm the land. From the cabin windows of today's jetliners the country might appear a two-tone, pasture and forest green but, on the ground, city and townscape dominate the lives of most New Zealanders.

PLATE 10. Coastal cliffs, Castlepoint

Akaroa on Banks Peninsula. The quaint little French colonial cottages, with delicate wrought-iron balconies and shuttered windows, are reminders of the half-hearted attempt to establish a French colony in the late 1830s.

Old woolshed now preserved in Masterton as an historic example of early Wairarapa farm buildings.

There are now three million New Zealanders and two-thirds of them live in just thirteen North Island and five South Island cities and towns. With the exception of a handful of latterday farming and timber towns, the main population centres are on the coast and were founded during the early colonial period. In the 1880s, with refrigeration's heady stimulus, their growth really began, gradually turning them into bustling ports and processing centres and — more recently — the focal points for fast-growing secondary industries.

Since early this century there has been a steady drift of population to the North Island, following the grassing of the north's hill country to capitalise on the new overseas markets. There has been a parallel drift to the cities from the villages and small towns that sprang up during the gold rushes, that huddled around dairy factories or straggled along through roads as they thrived in the service of surrounding farmers.

Opposite: Beech Forest in the lower Hollyford Valley on the way to Milford Sound.

PLATE 11. Mt Cook from Kea Point

River fishing for trout.

Opposite: From mountains to the sea, rivers now run the gauntlet of fertiliser run-off, chemical wastes, factory effluent and domestic sewerage. The upper reaches of the Wanganui River.

Today, New Zealand's cities sprawl over vast areas, mostly because urban New Zealanders retain something of their pioneering great-grandparents' stubborn independence, preferring to throw up lawn and shrub moats around their suburban castles than live in inner-city apartment buildings.

In Auckland, particularly, the suburbs and satellite cities seem never ending. The country's largest city, with three-quarters-of-a-million residents, has a large Maori community which is expanding at twice the European rate, quite recovered from the alarming musket and measles ravages of last century. Every year Auckland swallows another 808 ha (2,000 acres) of fertile farmland for housing and industry.

Not only do the cities spread in unadventurous conformity, but a voracious urban appetite has been largely responsible for the neck-to-neck race between electricity consumption and capacity, both doubling each decade during the last thirty years.

Most of the country's power is generated by hydro-electric schemes — the giant pylons seven-league booting it across country to towns and cities from the string of dams harnessing the major North and South Island rivers.

Hydro power schemes have also generated the most environmental concern in recent years. A decade's on-and-off plan to raise the level of Fiordland's isolated Lake Manapouri was buried by the public's largest-ever petition to Parliament. The eighty feet increase, necessary to supply the ultimate power requirements of the Bluff aluminium smelter, would have drowned many of the outstandingly beautiful lake's thirty-six islands and sandy beaches as well as the dense bush that tumbles down to the water's edge.

Lake Manapouri: no longer threatened?

64

PLATE 12. Morning mists, Hollyford Valley

Of course, the hopefully averted damage to Lake Manapouri and the still likely Clutha River valley flooding are only two of the more dramatic examples of the environmental side effects of nearly half-a-century's hydro-electric development. Dammed and diverted rivers have upset fish breeding patterns, artificial lakes have submerged 130 square kilometres (50 square miles) of land, river control systems have eliminated awe-inspiring waterfalls and rapids, bulldozers have scraped the ground bare for construction sites and short-lived towns.

At the same time, the hydro power planners won an environmental award in 1974 for the Waitaki River valley development.

The 78 square kilometres (30 square mile) man-made lake at Benmore, where trout prosper and boating enthusiasts spend weekends, has

Cromwell in Central Otago: possible victim of a hydro-electric power scheme.

transformed a brown, barren landscape. The surrounding hills are now greener, trees are growing, and visitors claim the climate is several degrees warmer. At Aviemore nearly half a million carefully-chosen trees have been planted, a fish-spawning race built, a natural habitat created for native swamp birds, and moa hunter camp remains and Maori rock drawings salvaged.

Perhaps the greatest danger to New Zealand's landscape is the compact diversity of climate and scenery which delights Australian, American and Japanese tourists who can flit, a day at a time, from deserted North Island moonscapes guarded by smoking volcanoes to Central Otago's rocky gorges, tumbling rivers and glimpses of crumbling gold-miner cottages; from the boiling mud and acrobatic geysers of the

Rangitikei River.

Shellfish gatherers — a rare sight now that the beds are depleted.

Rotorua thermal region to glaciers spilling into primitive Westland forests. .

Most New Zealanders live within sight of blue-tinted mountain ranges and the sound of surf beating out its hypnotic sea shore rythms. All year long New Zealand's accommodating landscape is playground for the enthusiastic inheritors of sometimes obsessive British sporting traditions. At holiday time the country closes down while New Zealanders take to the sea, bush or mountains.

Hundreds of thousands prescribe themselves annual sea, sand and sun tonics at the beach. Thousands more, particularly on Auckland's Waitemata Harbour and Hauraki Gulf, sail sleek keelers or just potter around in boats.

PLATE 13. North Taranaki coastline

Launches in Milford Sound.

Echoes of the sailing era, before diesel engines and oil slicks. A sailing scow at Collingwood, Golden Bay.

Hinemoa's pool on Mokoia Island in the middle of Lake Rotorua. The beautiful Hinemoa, living on the lake shore, fell in love with the son of a lesser chief on Mokoia Island. The match was forbidden by Hinemoa's chieftain father, but one night, hypnotised by Tutanekai's lilting flute music carrying across the water, she swam the mile to the island, reviving in the warm thermal pool. Today the lake that united the lovers is being smothered by weed.

Others tramp along bush trails, ski on the South Island's glacier fields, hunt deer and wild pig in the high country, or cut mountaineering teeth on the Alps' jagged peaks.

New Zealand packs a whole world of tourist and recreational attractions into three small islands. There is simply not room to absorb or deflect the mounting pressures of water, air and visual pollution.

It is not enough for this generation of New Zealanders to hope that others — central government, departments of state and local bodies — will solve these problems. Overseas experience suggests that continuous, well-organised campaigns by committed individuals and groups will be necessary to keep the public informed and stir the consciences of community and business leaders.

New Zealanders must actively promote more rigorous enforcement of pollution legislation, less milling of the native timbers, more curbs on a fast-growing population, more effort to save almost extinct bird species, more selective use of fertilisers and insecticides.

The alternative is indifference and expediency — and a gradual destruction of New Zealand's uniquely varied landscape.

Old, deserted cars, monuments to indifference,
are often countryside eyesores.

PLATE 15. Mt Ruapehu, Tongariro National Park

Don Neilson's Greytown garden.

A corner of Don Neilson's Greytown garden. The trees and shrubs were carefully chosen to encourage the greatest variety of native and introduced bird life. At least fifteen species come and go, adding variety to the chorus of early morning song and controlling the garden's insect population. Some of these birds are shown on the endpapers.

Magpie

Shining Cuckoo

Fantail

Goldfinch

Californian Quail

Chaffinch

Warbler